ACKNOWLEDGEMENT

Am extremely grateful to all mighty God, for all his goodness, love, provisions, protection and mercy toward my life and family, I return all glory to his name. This book would not be complete if I fail to recognize the effort of my dear sister who have contributed a good quota to the writing of this book. More to say, I appreciate the knowledge of good and great authors who have also contributed greatly to the publishing of this book. I cease this opportunity to say thank you.

DEDICATION

I dedicate this book to the almighty God, because all things worketh good and perfect through his love and power. Also to many who are seeking for the "Title of this book".

INTRODUCTION

One of the most important key steps to achieve success in life is knowing the meaning of success for one's life. The true meaning of success goes far beyond the common definitions of success, such as having a lot of money, being wealthy, having a lot of tangibles and earned degrees. Quite the opposite: true success in life cannot be measured with the above named factors, but instead with the amount of people that are able to live a better and more advanced life because of what you created. This is the meaning of success. Not the trophies people are collecting in their lives. Media and society lets us often conclude that living a successful life means to be extraordinarily wealthy and have a lot of tangibles. But the meaning of success is to live a happily life and to make this world a better place for everyone.

SECTIONS.

Section one: TIPS FOR SUCCESS

Understanding personality and character ethics.

The power of Paradigms.

The power of paradigm shift.

Seeing and Being.

Section two: HABIT OF SUCCESSFUL PEOPLE.

7 Habit of Successful people. (Others are essential)

Other factor for successful living

UNDERSTANDING PERSONALITY AND CHARACTER ETHICS .

The view of success shifted from the Character Ethic to what we might call the Personality Ethic. Success became more a function of personality, of public image, of attitudes and behaviors, skills and techniques that lubricate the processes of human interaction.

This Personality Ethic essentially took two paths: one was human and public relations techniques, and the other was positive mental attitude (PMA).

Some of this philosophy was expressed in inspiring and sometimes valid maxims such as "Your attitude".

THE POWER OF A PARADIGM.

The 7 Habits of Highly Effective People embody many of the fundamental principles of human effectiveness. These habits are basic; they are primary. They represent the internalization of correct principles upon which enduring happiness and success are based.

But before we can really understand these Seven Habits, we need to understand our own "paradigms" and how to make a "paradigm shift." model, theory, perception, assumption, or frame of reference. In the more general sense, it's the way we "see" the world not in terms of our visual sense of sight, but in terms of perceiving, understanding, and interpreting.

For our purposes, a simple way to understand paradigms is to see them as maps. We all know that "the map is not the territory." A map is simply an explanation of certain aspects of the territory. That's exactly what a paradigm is. It is a theory, an explanation, or model of something else.

A paradigm is the ways you "see," interpret, or understand the world.

THE POWER OF PARADIGM SHIFT.

Perhaps the most important insight to be gained from the perception demonstration is in the area of paradigm shifting, what we might call the "Aha!" experience when someone finally "sees" the composite picture in another way. The more bound a person is by the initial perception, the more powerful the "Aha!" experience is. It's as though a light were suddenly turned on inside.

SEEING AND BEING.

Of course, not all paradigm shifts are instantaneous. Unlike the instant insight on the subway, the paradigm shifting experience gotten from the story between Sandra and Marcus with our son was slow, difficult, and deliberate process. The approach they had first taken with him was the outgrowth of years of conditioning and experience in the Personality Ethic. It was the result of deeper paradigms they held about Their success as parents as well as the measure of success of our children.

Principles are not practices. A practice is a specific activity or action. A practice that works in one circumstance will not necessarily work in other circumstances, as parents who have tried to raise a second child exactly like they did the first can readily attest.

While practices are situationally specific, principles are deep, fundamental truths that have universal application. They apply to individuals, to marriages, to families, to private and public organizations of every kind. When these truths are internalized into habits, they empower people to create a wide variety of practices to deal with different situations.

Principles are not values. A gang of thieves can share values, but they are in violation of the fundamental principles we're talking about. Principles are the territory. Values are maps. When we value correct principles, we have truth and knowledge of things as they are.

Principles are guidelines for human conduct that are proven to have enduring, permanent value. They're fundamental. They're essentially unarguable because they are self-evident. One way to quickly grasp the selfevident nature of principles is to simply consider the absurdity of attempting to live an effective life based on their opposites. I doubt that anyone would seriously consider unfairness, deceit, baseness, uselessness, mediocrity, or degeneration to be a solid foundation for lasting happiness and success. Although people may argue about how these principles are defined or manifested or achieved, there seems to be an innate consciousness and awareness that they exist.

The more closely our maps or paradigms are aligned with these principles or natural laws, the more accurate and functional they will be. Correct maps will infinitely impact our personal and interpersonal effectiveness far more than any amount of effort expended on changing our attitudes and behaviors.

HABIT OF SUCCESSFUL PEOPLE.

1. Organization

One of the most frequently mentioned habits of those who are successful in life is organization. Such organization includes planning as well as setting priorities and goals.

Have a "To-Do List" every evening before going to bed to prepare for the next day, is one of the ladder to being successful in life.

2. Relaxation.

It's interesting to note that relaxing by meditating or simply avoiding distractions is another of the most-often mentioned habits of successful people.

Of course, relaxation comes more easily to those who are organized, so perhaps for some, it is more of a natural byproduct than a conscious decision.

It may also be that the act of "taking a breath" is the successful person's way of preparing for the effort yet to come. In fact, one of the first steps toward achieving a meditative or relaxed state is to concentrate on your own breathing for three to five minutes.

3. **Taking Action.**

Third on the list of habits of successful people is the inevitable "action" habit. It is important to organize, to plan, and to set priorities, but without action, a plan is nothing more than potential.

Successful people act quickly and often. In addition, although it may sound counterintuitive, according to James Clear, they act (start, anyway) before they feel ready.

While others come up with reasons not to act, successful people take that all important first step even if it seems outlandish.

4. **Personal Care.**

Personal care with regard to diet, exercise, and hygiene comes next on the list of habits of those who are successful.

For some, personal care involves a complex regimen and a highly disciplined lifestyle. For others, not so much. Elon Musk, the CEO of Tesla Motors, put it succinctly when asked what daily habit has had the largest positive impact on his life. Musk said simply, "Showering."

5. **Positive Attitude.**

According to many successful people, having a positive attitude is not just a result of being successful. it's one of the root causes of success.

Joel Brown refers to gratitude and positive self-talk as priorities in the lives of the ultra successful. Moreover, Brown says, it's not enough to express gratitude and a positive attitude. You must also remind yourself why you are grateful in order to achieve a deeper effect.

6. **Networking.**

Successful people know the value of exchanging ideas with others through networking. They also know the value of collaboration and teamwork all of which are likely when you network.

Successful people know the importance of surrounding themselves with other successful people, according to author Thomas Corley. Corley says 79% of wealthy people spend at least five hours a month networking.

7. **Frugality.**

Frugal is not the same as stingy. Frugality is a habit of being thrifty, with money and resources. It is also a habit of being economical. Learning to be economical comes through avoiding waste, which automatically results in efficiency.

Successful people avoid overspending. Instead, they comparison-shop and negotiate. The result is financial success through the simple act of saving more money than they spend.

OTHER FACTORS FOR SUCCESSFUL LIVING

(i). **Rising Early.**

The more time one can devote to being successful, the more likely success will result. Successful people are accustomed to rising early, and that habit appears repeatedly among those who do well in life.

While the "Early Riser's Club" has a huge membership among successful people, a few notable members include Sir Richard Branson of Virgin Group, former Disney CEO Robert Iger and former Yahoo! CEO Marissa Mayer.

(ii). **Sharing the little knowledge you have.**

Whether through donating to charity or the sharing of ideas, successful people have a habit of giving. They know the value of sharing and most believe their success should result in something more than the accumulation of wealth for themselves.

Lack of wealth does not need to be a factor when it comes to sharing. Volunteering in your community or at a local school does not cost anything but could provide help where it is needed most.

(iii). **Reading.**

It's important to note that successful people read. While they also read for pleasure, most use their reading habit as a means to gain knowledge or insight.

For anyone who needs inspiration about the value and importance of reading, look no further than the example of billionaire author, J.K. Rowling, who says she read "anything" as a child. She advises, "Read as much as you possibly can. Nothing will help you as much as reading."

(iv) **Passion**

When your heart beats for a certain cause, you're undefeatable. Passion is a guarantee that you'll still persevere when things get tough and that as long as it takes to be successful.

(v). **Authenticity**

Don't waste your time maintaining an image of yourself that the people around you like but that's not who you are. It will cost you too much energy in the long run that you actually need for your success. Just be yourself and make the most of your strengths that's convincing.

(vi). **Optimism**

Is the glass half empty or half full? The right perspective is key. If you go through life with optimism, you can motivate yourself much better for success.

(vii). **Empathy**

Can you empathize with your counterpart? If so, you have a clear advantage because the sense of expectations and emotions of others is very helpful and allows you to reach consensus more easily with others.

(viii) **Openness.**

There is a lot of change, especially in this day and age. If you are not open to change, you will at some point not be able to participate actively, regardless of how intelligent you are. Being open to new things and new challenges, on the other hand, makes it possible to react quickly to change and in some cases to be able to use it to your advantage.

(ix) **Support**

In difficult situations, support from your social

surroundings helps you to overcome setbacks and master challenges. Knowing that you won't be left alone, even if you fail, you can find the path to success much more freely.

(x) **Communication skills**

"You can get help only if you ask," an old saying goes. And it's true: If you communicate with others, you can achieve a lot. Take the initiative and speak to others about what you would like to achieve. That's how you'll reach your goal.

(xi) **Motivation**

Motivation is what lets you keep going and drives you to be successful. If you can motivate yourself well, nothing can stop you.

(xii) **Willingness to learn**

Staying at the same level of knowledge means that others will pass you by at some point. If you're lacking skills, you can certainly acquire them by learning. Be prepared to continue learning and accept advice and information from others.

(xiii) **Courage**

On the path to success, you often have to make decisions that are difficult because they find little favour in your environment or because they're connected with financial risk. If you're courageous, you'll be able to make these decisions against all obstacles "Nothing ventured, nothing gained."

(xiv) **Resilience**

Resilience is the ability to cope well with pressure and stress situations. Mistakes are nothing to be ashamed of but rather a chance to learn and do better the next time.

(xv) **Discipline**

If you want to be successful, you have to hang in there. That works only with discipline. Are you prepared to work on your success every day and to remain persistent even when things become taxing?

(xvi) **Confidence**

You believe in your success and can communicate that?

Appearing confident will impress those around you and helps you be perceived as successful, thus making the path to success easier to pursue.

(xvii) **Sense of responsibility**

Taking responsibility for your own decisions and actions is important to continuing your development. If you don't do that, at some point, you won't get ahead anymore despite smarts.

(xviii) **Patience**

"Good things come to those who wait" With a little patience, you can be much more successful in the long run. Be prepared to wait a little longer for success. That will make it possible for you to approach decisions with a much greater foresight.

SUMMARY

People have habits some are positive, some are not. Successful people tend to have more of the kinds of habits that contribute to their success. The good news, for those who wish to be successful, is that cultivating positive habits takes no more effort than developing bad ones.

www.ingramcontent.com/pod-product-compliance
Lightning Source LLC
Chambersburg PA
CBHW061330140726
47998CB00007B/2640